Space

Tim Clifford

Rourke
Publishing LLC
Vero Beach, Florida 32964

www.rourkepublishing.com

PHOTO CREDITS: Title Page: © Karl Dolenc; Page 5: © Diego Barucco; Page 6: © NASA; Page 7: © Andreas Guskos; Page 8-9: © NASA; Page 10: © Simon Gurney; Page 11: © Sebastian Kaulitzki, George Toubalis; Page 12: © Sebastian Kaulitzki; Page 13: © Sebastian Kaulitzki; Page 15: © Kris Hanke, Mario Tarello; Page 16: © René Mansi; Page 17: © Xavier Gallego, Hans-Walter Untch, Igor Zhorov, Mario Hornik; Page 18: © Sebastian Kaulitzki; Page 20: © George Toubalis; Page 21: © NASA; Page 22: © Matteo Natale, George Toubalis; Page 24: © George Toubalis; Page 26: © NASA, George Toubalis; Page 27: © NASA; Page 28: © NASA, George Toubalis; Page 29: © NASA; Page 30: © NASA, George Toubalis; Page 31: © NASA; Page 32: © NASA, George Toubalis; Page 33: © NASA; Page 34: © NASA, George Toubalis; Page 36: © George Toubalis; Page 37: © Phil Hart, Kenneth C. Zirkel; Page 38: © NASA; Page 39: © Stephan Hoerold; Page 40: © Paul LeFevre; Page 41: © NASA; Page 42: © Paul LeFevre; Page 43: © Thomas Tuchan, Manfred Konrad; Page 44: © NASA

Editor: Robert Stengard-Olliges

Cover design by Nicky Stratford, bdpublishing.com

Library of Congress Cataloging-in-Publication Data

Clifford, Tim, 1959-
 Space / Tim Clifford.
    p. cm. -- (Let's explore science)
 ISBN 978-1-60044-624-5
1. Outer space--Juvenile literature. I. Title.
QB500.22.C62 2008
520--dc22

                                    2007019663

Printed in the USA

CG/CG

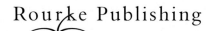

Rourke Publishing

www.rourkepublishing.com – rourke@rourkepublishing.com
Post Office Box 3328. Vero Beach. FL 32964

CONTENTS

CHAPTER 1   **What Is Outer Space?**   4

CHAPTER 2   **The Solar System**   8

CHAPTER 3   **The Earth's Place**

               in Space   10

CHAPTER 4   **The Moon**   14

CHAPTER 5   **The Sun**   18

CHAPTER 6   **The Eight Planets**   20

CHAPTER 7   **Other Objects**

               in Space   36

Time Line of Space Exploration   **44**

Websites to Visit/Further Reading   **45**

Glossary   **46**

Index   **48**

CHAPTER ONE

WHAT IS OUTER SPACE?

What do you think of when you hear the word "space?" You might think of the Sun and the **planets** in our **solar system**. You might picture the billions of **stars** that light up the sky at night, or **asteroids** and meteors as they hurtle through the sky. All of these are part of our incredibly vast **universe**.

The solar system including dwarf planet Pluto and the asteroid belt.

Gases and dust gathering south of the constellation Orion's belt.

When people talk of space, they usually mean **outer space**, which is the area of space beyond the Earth's **atmosphere**. In the United States, anyone who flies beyond an altitude of 50 miles (80.5 km) is considered to be an **astronaut**.

An astronaut on a spacewalk with the Earth in the background.

The farther you go from the Earth's surface, the thinner the atmosphere becomes. As you travel higher, there is less and less air. As you reach outer space, there is almost no air, or anything else. Outer space is mostly empty.

Looking down on Earth's surface from a higher atmosphere.

CHAPTER TWO

THE SOLAR SYSTEM

Mercury

Venus

Earth

Mars

Jupiter

Ceres

To begin to understand space, we first need to know what is in our own neighborhood. In Earth's case, our neighborhood is called the solar system. This is made up of the Sun and all the planets and objects that revolve around it. The Sun is at the center of our solar system.

Eight planets orbit, or revolve around, the Sun. These planets are Mercury, Venus, Earth, Mars, Jupiter, Saturn, Uranus, and Neptune.

Many of these planets have at least one **moon**. Moons are

Saturn

Uranus

Neptune

CHAPTER THREE

THE EARTH'S PLACE IN SPACE

A sea turtle swimming in the ocean.

The Earth is unique in the solar system because it is the only planet that we know where life is supported. Animals and plants are abundant. You can see them everywhere! Even the oceans are filled with life.

Our planet supports life because of its position in the solar system. At an average distance of about 93 million miles (150 million km), we are the third planet from the Sun. Our temperatures and our atmosphere create perfect conditions for life forms to thrive.

The Earth travels around the Sun in an elliptical, or oval, orbit. We are never closer than 91.5 million miles (147.3 million km) from the Sun, or farther than 94.5 million miles (152 million km). This helps keep the Earth from getting too hot or too cold.

The Earth revolves, or goes completely around, the Sun once every 365.25 days. That is how we measure years— one trip around the Sun equals one Earth year.

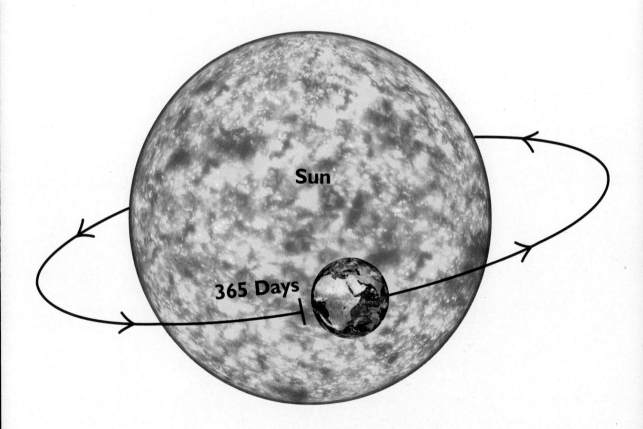

The Earth itself rotates, or spins, in space as it travels around the Sun. It takes about 24 hours, or one day, for the Earth to rotate completely on its **axis**. Because the Earth rotates, each part of the Earth spins toward and away from the light of the Sun. This is what creates day and night.

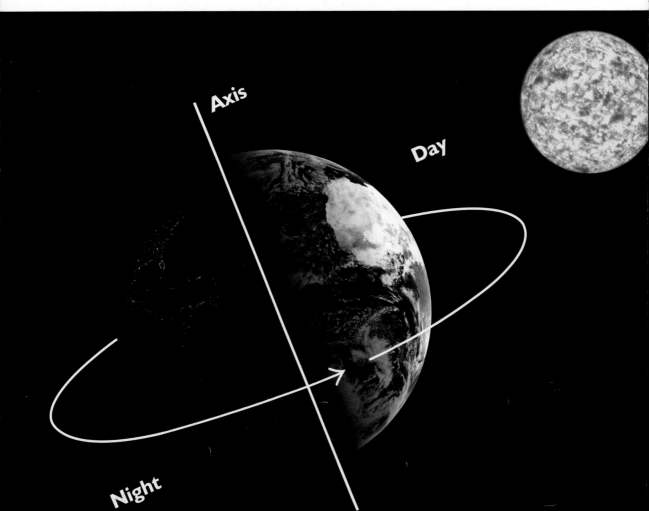

Axis

Day

Night

The Earth tilts on its axis about 23.5 degrees. As it revolves around the Sun in the course of a year, this tilt causes some parts of the Earth to tilt toward the Sun and other parts to tilt away from the Sun. This creates the seasons.

When the northern hemisphere, or half, of the Earth is tilted toward the Sun, the southern hemisphere is tilted away. When it is summer in the northern hemisphere, it is winter in the southern hemisphere, and vice versa.

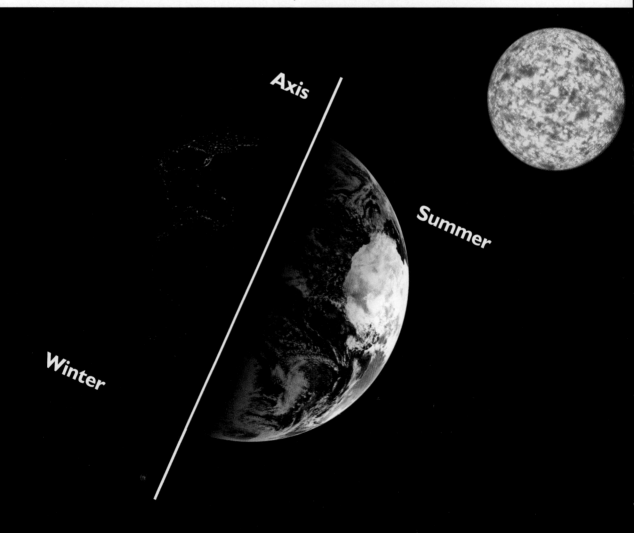

CHAPTER FOUR

THE MOON

Apart from the Sun, the Earth's Moon is the largest object we can see in the sky. It is the closest object to us in the solar system, yet it is still about 240,000 miles (386,200 km) away!

A view of the Moon from Earth.

The Moon is covered in craters, which are large bowl-shaped holes in the surface of the Moon caused by collisions with objects such as meteorites.

As a satellite of the Earth, the Moon orbits the Earth once every 29.5 days, or about once a month. In a single month, we are able to see the Moon in many different phases.

The phases of the Moon, called **lunar phases**, refer to how the Moon appears to people on Earth. Half of the Moon is always illuminated by the Sun. As the Moon orbits the Earth, however, we don't always see that entire half. At each phase, a different part of the Moon is visible.

The Moon as it orbits the Earth.

Lunar Phases

In a waxing moon, the visible part of the Moon is getting larger. In a waning moon, the visible part of the Moon is getting smaller.

New Moon

Waxing Crescent Moon

First Quarter Moon

Waxing Gibbous Moon

Full Moon

Waning Gibbous Moon

Last Quarter Moon

Waning Crescent Moon

Have you ever had to move farther back at the beach because the water seemed to be coming closer and closer? What you experienced was the rising **tide** of the ocean.

Tides are caused by the gravitational pull of the Sun and Moon on the water, and are most affected by the Moon because it is so close to us. The points on Earth closest to and opposite the Moon experience high tides. The further you go from those points, the lower the tide.

Low Tide

High Tide

Before people understood how the solar system worked, they were terrified of **eclipses**! People thought that an eclipse was a sign of bad luck or evil. We now know that an eclipse is the blocking of the light of one celestial body, such as the Sun or the Moon, by another celestial body. The eclipses we see on Earth always involve the Moon.

In a lunar eclipse, the light of the Moon is blocked by some part of the Earth's shadow. In a solar eclipse, the Moon blocks the Earth's view of the Sun. If the Sun or Moon becomes totally invisible, it is called a total eclipse. This is the rarest kind. Most eclipses leave some of the Sun or Moon visible. They are called partial eclipses.

Lunar Eclipse

Solar Eclipse

CHAPTER FIVE

THE SUN

Until about 500 years ago, most people thought that the Earth was the center of the universe and the Sun and other planets revolved around it. This was called the *geocentric* model of the universe.

We now know that the Sun is at the center of our solar system, a belief that was proposed by the Polish astronomer Nikolai Copernicus in 1543. This is called the *heliocentric* model, named after the Greek sun god Helios.

The Sun is a medium sized star in the Milky Way galaxy, one of billions of such stars in the universe. It is a yellow dwarf star. Despite that name, the Sun is by far the largest body in our solar system. The Earth has a diameter of almost 8,000 miles (12,870 km), but the Sun's diameter is over 1,000 times larger!

Because of its great size, the Sun exerts great gravitational pull on the planets that keep them in orbit.

Even though the Sun is far from Earth, it supplies almost all the heat and energy on our planet. It does this by burning gases that reach temperatures of 11,000° F (6,093° C) on the surface. Temperatures can reach 27 million° F (15 million° C) at the Sun's core.

Facts about the Sun

Astronomical symbol:

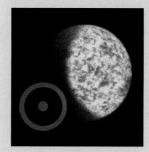

A circle with a dot inside.

Contains 98 percent of the mass of the entire solar system.

4.5 billion years old.

Made mostly of hydrogen and helium.

Also called Sol (Latin) and Helios (Greek).

You should never look directly into the Sun, even during an eclipse.

The Sun provides energy for life on Earth.

CHAPTER SIX

THE EIGHT PLANETS

A planet is any of the large bodies that orbit the Sun, including Mercury, Venus, Earth, Mars, Jupiter, Saturn, Uranus, and Neptune, in order of closeness to the Sun.

Mercury

Mercury is the first of the four **terrestrial planets**. This means it is a planet made mostly of rock. The planets closest to the Sun—Venus, Earth, and Mars—are the other three.

Mercury is the smallest of the terrestrial planets. It has an iron core that accounts for about 3/4 of its diameter. Most of the rest of the planet is made up of a rocky crust.

Because it is so close to the Sun, it is very difficult to see Mercury. A NASA mission called Messenger is expected to begin orbiting the planet in 2011. It is expected that this will help us learn a great deal more about this rarely seen planet.

The Messenger launched on the Boeing Delta II rocket on August 3, 2004. It will reach Mercury on March 18, 2011.

Facts about Mercury

Astronomical Symbol:

Mercury's winged helmet.

Origin of name:
Mercury was a god in Roman mythology. He was a messenger with winged feet.

Diameter:
3,032 miles (4,879 km).

Distance from Sun:
28.5 to 43 million miles (45.9 to 69 million km).

Length of year:
88 days.

Number of Moons:
None.

Venus

Of all the planets, Venus is the one most similar to Earth. In fact, Venus is often called Earth's "sister" planet. As similar as it is in some ways, however, it is also very different in others.

Earth and Venus are similar in size. The two planets are very close to each other as they orbit the Sun; because of this, Venus is the most visible planet in the night sky. Both planets are relatively young, judging from the lack of craters on their surfaces.

We now know that the environment on Venus couldn't support life as Earth does. Our atmosphere is a breathable mix of oxygen and other gases, but the atmosphere on Venus is mostly carbon dioxide, which is a poisonous gas. The temperature on Earth rarely goes much higher than 100° F (37.8° C), even at the equator, but the temperature on the surface of Venus can exceed 850° F (454° C)!

The atmosphere of Venus would be compared to the exhaust from a car.

The Earth is mostly water, but whatever water that may have existed once on Venus has boiled away due to the intense heat.

Facts about Venus

Astronomical Symbol:

The same as the gender symbol for female.

Origin of name:
Venus was the Roman goddess of love and beauty.

Diameter:
7,520 miles (12,100 km).

Distance from Sun:
About 67 million miles (108 million km).

Length of year:
225 days.

Number of Moons:
None.

Earth

The Earth is the only planet known where life exists. Almost 1.5 million species of animals and plants have been discovered so far, and many more have yet to be found. While other planets may have small amounts of ice or steam, the Earth is 2/3 water. Earth has perfect conditions for a breathable atmosphere.

Earth is the largest of the terrestrial planets and the fifth largest in the solar system. It is believed to be about 4.5 billion years old, which makes it very young compared to other celestial bodies!

A pair of Elks with calf drinking water from the Madison River.

Facts about Earth

Astronomical Symbol:

A circle with an equator and a meridian line at right angles.

Origin of name:
Probably from the Old English word that means "soil."

Diameter:
7,926 miles (12,755 km).

Distance from Sun:
93 million miles
(150 million km).

Length of year:
365 days.

Number of Moons:
One.

Mars

No planet has sparked the imaginations of humans as much as Mars. It may be the reddish color of Mars, or the fact that it can often be easily seen in the night sky, that has caused people to wonder about this close neighbor of ours. Tales of "Martians" invading Earth have been around for well over fifty years. But is it likely that any kind of life really does exist on Mars?

Scientists aren't sure. Life as we know it couldn't survive there. Even so, there is evidence that there may be water on Mars. The presence of methane, which may be given off by organisms, provides another clue.

Does this all mean you need to be concerned about an alien attack from Mars? Hardly. Still, as we learn more and more about the final terrestrial planet, the more mysterious and wonderful Mars becomes.

One of the first images taken from the Mars Pathfinder when it landed on Mars on July 4, 1997.

Deimos

Phobos

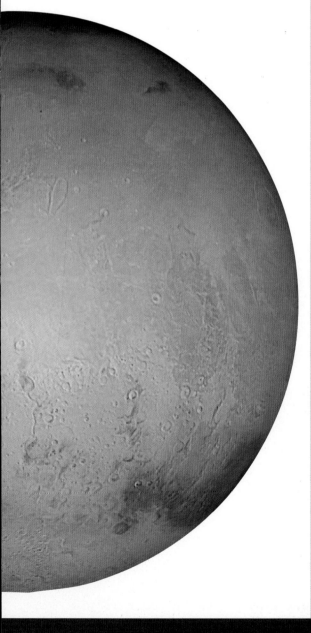

Facts about Mars

Astronomical Symbol:

The gender symbol for male.

Origin of name:
Named after Mars, the Roman god of war, perhaps because of the planet's red color.

Diameter:
4,217 miles (6,786 km).

Distance from the Sun:
142 million miles
(229 million km).

Length of year:
687 days.

Number of Moons:
Two, called Deimos and Phobos.

Jupiter

The planet Jupiter is the first of the **gas giant** planets. Made mostly of gas, they include Jupiter, Saturn, Uranus, and Neptune.

Jupiter is first among the planets in terms of size and mass. Its diameter is 11 times bigger than Earth, and its mass is 2.5 times greater than all the other planets combined. The "Great Red Spot" on Jupiter is actually a raging storm.

This giant planet comes in first again when it comes to giving off heat. The core of Jupiter may be made of liquid rock that reaches temperatures of 43,000° F (23,870° C).

There are at least 63 moons of different sizes orbiting Jupiter. That's the most of any planet. Its largest moon is called Ganymede. It has a diameter of 3,400 miles (5,472 km)—larger than Mercury!

Great Red Spot

Ganymede

Lo

Europa

Callisto

Facts about Jupiter

Astronomical Symbol:

Origin of name:
Named after Jupiter, the principal god in Roman mythology.

Diameter:
88,732 miles (142,800 km).

Distance from Sun:
484 million miles
(779 million km).

Length of year:
Almost 12 Earth years.

Number of Moons:
63.

Saturn

Most people know about the rings around Saturn, because they are the brightest and most colorful. These rings are made mainly out of ice particles orbiting the planet. While the rings themselves seem big, the particles are very small, usually no more than 10 feet (3 meters) wide.

Saturn is the second largest planet. It is the farthest planet from the Earth that can be seen without a telescope. It appears flat at the poles because its great rotational speed makes the middle of the planet bulge.

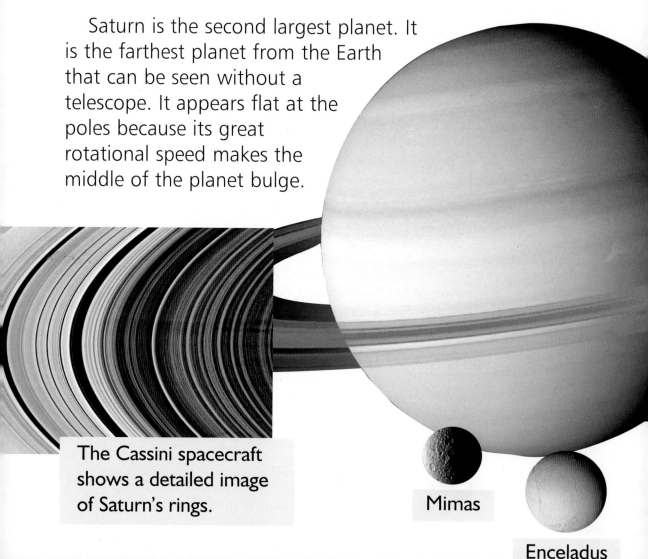

The Cassini spacecraft shows a detailed image of Saturn's rings.

Mimas

Enceladus

Titan

Rhea

Dione

Tethys

Facts about Saturn

Astronomical Symbol:

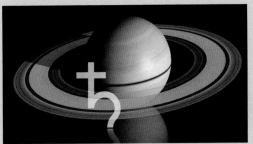

Believed to represent the scythe of the god Saturn.

Origin of name:
Saturn was the ancient Roman god of agriculture.

Diameter:
74,900 miles (120,537 km).

Distance from Sun:
888 million miles
(14,290 million km).

Length of year:
29.5 Earth years.

Number of Moons:
At least 56.

Uranus

Uranus is the first planet so far away from the Earth that it can only be seen with the use of a telescope. When it was first discovered in 1781, scientists didn't know what they had found. As astronomers studied the object more closely, they discovered that it had a circular orbit around the Sun. They had found the seventh planet.

Uranus is so far from the Sun that it takes 84 years to complete an orbit of the Sun. It is the only planet that spins on its side, so each pole is tilted away from the Sun for half its orbit. That means each night and day lasts an amazing 42 years. Imagine staying awake that long! Of course, you'd also get a lot of time to catch up on your sleep!

The Hubble telescope captured this image of Uranus with its rings and some of its moons.

Miranda

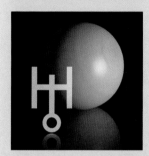

Facts about Uranus

Astronomical Symbol:

Origin of name:
Comes from Ouranos, the Greek word for "sky."

Diameter:
About 32,200 miles (51,819 km).

Distance from Sun:
1,783,940,000 miles (2,870,894,600 km).

Length of year:
84 Earth years.

Number of Moons:
21.

Neptune

Imagine being so good at math that you could figure out the location of a planet you had never even seen! That is what John C. Adams did in 1843 when he discovered Neptune.

Neptune was named after the Roman god of the sea because it is so far out in the deep "sea" of space. The name also fits because Neptune appears to be a beautiful bright blue because of the methane clouds that surround it.

It is the most distant planet from the Sun. It takes a very long time—165 years—to orbit the Sun. Neptune has made only one trip around the Sun since it was discovered.

The Voyager 2 launched on a Titan/Centaur rocket on August 20, 1977 and approached Neptune on August 25, 1989.

Facts about Neptune

Astronomical Symbol:

Neptune's trident.

Origin of name:
Ancient Roman god of the sea, often pictured holding a trident (a spear with three sharp prongs).

Diameter:
30,777 miles (49,529 km).

Distance from Sun:
2,795,084,800 miles (4,498,033,400 km).

Length of year:
About 165 Earth years.

Number of Moons:
13.

CHAPTER SEVEN

OTHER OBJECTS IN SPACE

There are many other objects in our solar system as well as the planets and their moons.

Dwarf Planets

There used to be nine planets, and now there are only eight! Did one explode? Did it fly out of the solar system? No, all that happened was that in 2006 scientists decided that Pluto wasn't big enough to be considered a true planet. Pluto has become one of the three known dwarf planets.

Pluto

A dwarf planet is a planet smaller than Mercury. Currently known dwarf planets include Pluto, Ceres, and Eris. Other dwarf planets may yet be discovered in the **Kuiper Belt**, a band of small bodies orbiting the Sun beyond Neptune.

Comets

Years ago, when a **comet** streaked across the sky like a giant fireball, people feared that disaster was about to strike. Some even thought that a comet was a sign that the world was about to end!

We now know that a comet is a ball of ice and dust particles that orbits the Sun. The particles following behind the comet are called its tail. We can only see comets when they are heated and lit up as they near the Sun.

Comet McNaught

The most famous comet is Halley's Comet, which can be seen every 76 years. Its next visit won't be until 2062!

Comet Hale-Bopp over Monument Valley, Arizona, March 1997.

Asteroids

Asteroids are small bodies that orbit the Sun like planets. They are sometimes called minor planets, and for a good reason. If you added up their total mass, they would be smaller than the Moon. Yet, there are hundreds of thousands of them. Most of them travel between the orbits of Mars and Jupiter in what is known as the asteroid belt.

The largest known asteroid is Ceres, which is also considered a dwarf planet. Yet even Ceres is tiny compared to a planet. Its diameter is only about 590 miles (950 km) across.

Asteroids Ida and Gaspra from the asteroid belt.

The dwarf planet Ceres taken by the Dawn spacecraft.

Meteoroids

A shooting star isn't really a star at all. It is the remains of a meteoroid, which is a small piece of debris in the solar system. Meteoroids are much smaller than asteroids; in fact, they are often formed from parts of asteroids that have broken apart. Some are believed to be parts of comets.

A meteor over downtown Portland.

When a meteoroid enters the Earth's atmosphere, it begins to burn up and glow. At that point, we call it a *meteor*, or what is often known as a "shooting star." Most meteors burn up completely before they ever hit the ground. Meteors that hit the Earth are called *meteorites*.

Barringer Crater in Arizona is also called the Meteor Crater.

Stars and Galaxies

The solar system is just a tiny part of outer space. Beyond our solar system lie billions of stars and **galaxies**.

Stars

Pleiades, also know as Seven Sisters constellation.

On a clear night, you can see stars speckling the sky in numbers far too large to count. No one knows exactly how many stars there are, but they far outnumber our ability to count them.

A star is a large, luminous ball of gas. Our Sun is a medium sized star. The distance between stars helps us begin to understand the vast size of the universe.

The star closest to our Sun is called Proxima Centauri. It is 4.22 **light years** away. A light year is the distance that light can travel in one year, or about 5.88 trillion miles (9.46 trillion km). Can you begin to see how incredibly large this universe of ours really is?

Like humans, stars have life cycles. Stars are born, they exist, and eventually they die. Let's look at the life cycle of a typical star.

The Life Cycle of a Star

STAGE ONE: *Birth*
Gases and dust gather in space, collapsing in from their own gravity as the star is born.

STAGE TWO: *Main Sequence*
Hydrogen is converted to helium through nuclear fusion, which supplies the star's energy.

STAGE THREE: *Red Giant*
The star uses up its hydrogen. It grows larger, cooler, and redder.

STAGE FOUR: *White Dwarf*
The red giant burns off its outer layers leaving mostly the core.

STAGE FIVE: *Death*
The white dwarf uses up all its energy and cools off to a black mass in space, called a black dwarf.

Sometimes, a large star dies in a spectacular explosion called a supernova. The material from such an explosion may help in the formation of new stars.

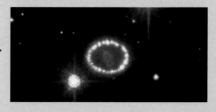

Galaxies

Andromeda Galaxy

Just as our solar system is a group of planets, a galaxy is a group of stars held together by gravity. Galaxies can contain anywhere from a few million to more than a trillion stars. The largest ones can be as much as a half million light years in diameter. There may be more than 100 billion galaxies in the universe.

With such a large universe, you might wonder where the Earth is located. We are in a galaxy called the Milky Way, which is a medium sized galaxy containing about 100 billion stars, including our own Sun.

Stephan's Quintet is a
group of five galaxies
including the Milky Way.

Triangulum Galaxy

Types of Galaxies

Spiral Galaxies

These galaxies
look like a bulging
plate with long,
winding arms.
The Milky Way is
a spiral galaxy.

Elliptical Galaxies

These galaxies
look round or
oval. They tend
to contain older
stars than
spiral galaxies.

Irregular Galaxies

These galaxies
don't have a
regular shape like
spiral and elliptical
galaxies do.

TIME LINE OF SPACE EXPLORATION

October 4, 1957

Sputnik 1 becomes the first artificial satellite to orbit the Earth.

May 5, 1961

Alan Shepard, Jr. becomes the first American in space aboard Freedom 7.

June 16, 1963

Valentina Tereshkova becomes the first woman in space aboard Vostok 6.

April 12, 1981

The space shuttle Columbia is launched. It is the first reusable manned spacecraft.

July 4, 1997

The unmanned Mars Pathfinder lands on Mars and conducts experiments.

April 12, 1961

Yuri Gagarin becomes the first human in space aboard Vostok 1.

February 20, 1962

John Glenn becomes the first American to orbit the Earth aboard Friendship 7.

July 20, 1969

Neil Armstrong and Buzz Aldrin become the first humans to land and walk on the Moon.

June 13, 1983

Pioneer 10, an unmanned spacecraft, passes Neptune. It is the first craft to leave our solar system.

August 15, 2006

Voyager 1, the most distant spacecraft in history, reaches 100 astronomical units from the Sun. That means that it has traveled 100 times as far from the Sun as the Earth is.

Questions to Consider

1. What are the four terrestrial planets? What are the four gas giants?

2. What features of the Earth make life possible on our planet?

3. List the planets according to their distance from the Sun. Next to each planet, list its diameter. Is there any relationship between a planet's size and its distance from the Sun? What is it?

Websites to Visit

http://spaceplace.nasa.gov/en/kids/
http://www.nasa.gov/audience/forkids/kidsclub/flash/index.html
http://www.nationalgeographic.com/solarsystem/splash.html

Further Reading

Carson, Mary Kay. *Exploring the Solar System: A History with 22 Activities*. Chicago Review Press, 2006.

Davis, Kenneth C. *Don't Know Much About the Solar System*. HarperTrophy, 2004.

Simon, Seymour. *Our Solar System*. (Revised Edition). Collins, 2007.

Visual Encyclopedia of Space. DK Publishing, 2006.

GLOSSARY

asteroids (AS tuh roids) — small bodies that orbit the Sun like planets

astronaut (AS troh nawt) — someone who travels in space

atmosphere (AT mohs feer) — the layer of gases surrounding the Earth

axis (AK sis) — an imaginary line on which a planet or other space object is said to rotate

comet (KAH meht) — a ball of ice and dust particles that orbits the Sun

dwarf planet (DWORF PLAN it) — a planet smaller than Mercury. Currently known dwarf planets include Pluto, Ceres, and Eris

eclipse (e KLIPS) — the blocking of the light of one celestial body, such as the Sun or the Moon, by another celestial body

galaxy (GAL ax see) — a system of stars held together by gravity

gas giant (GAS JIE uhnt) — one of the four large planets made mostly of gas. They include Jupiter, Saturn, Uranus, and Neptune

gravitational pull (grav ih TAY shun ul PUL) — the attraction one object exerts on another due to its mass

Kuiper Belt (KI per BELT) — a band of small bodies orbiting the Sun beyond Neptune

light year (LITE YEER) — the distance that light can travel in one year, or about 5.88 trillion miles (9.46 trillion km)

lunar phases (LOON er FAYZ es) — how the Moon appears to people on Earth

meteoroid (MEE tee uh roid) — a small piece of debris in the solar system

moon (MOON) — a natural satellite that orbits a planet

outer space (OW tur SPAYS) — the area of space beyond the Earth's atmosphere

planet (PLAN it) — any of the large bodies that orbit the Sun, including Mercury, Venus, Earth, Mars, Jupiter, Saturn, Uranus, and Neptune in order of closeness to the Sun

solar system (SOH lur SIS tuhm) — the Sun and all the planets and objects that revolve around it

star (STAHR) — a large, luminous ball of gas

terrestrial planet (tuh REST ree uhl PLAN it) — a planet made mostly of rock. These include Mercury, Venus, Earth, and Mars

tide (TIDE) — the rising and falling of the oceans and other bodies of water

universe (YOO nih vers) — all the matter and energy in space

INDEX

asteroids   4, 9, 38, 39
atmosphere   6, 7
axis   12, 13
comets   9, 37, 39
Copernicus   18
dwarf planets   9, 36, 38
eclipses   17
galaxy   18, 40, 42, 43
gas giant   28
geocentric   18
gravitational pull   9, 16, 19
Halley's Comet   37
heliocentric   18
Kuiper Belt   36
lunar phases   15

meteorites   14, 39
meteoroids   9, 39
meteors   4, 39
methane   26, 34
Milky Way   18, 42
orbit   11, 14, 20
outer space   6, 7
Proxima Centauri   40
solar system   4, 8, 10, 14, 17, 36, 39, 42
stars   40, 41
supernova   41
terrestrial planets   20, 24, 26
universe   4, 40, 42

About the Author

Tim Clifford is an education writer and the author of several children's books. He is a teacher who lives and works in New York City.